D1450573

BEARS

Giant Pandas

Stuart A. Kallen
ABDO & Daughters

visit us at
www.abdopub.com

Published by Abdo & Daughters, 4940 Viking Drive, Suite 622, Edina, Minnesota 55435.

Copyright © 1998 by Abdo Consulting Group, Inc., Pentagon Tower, P.O. Box 36036, Minneapolis, Minnesota 55435 USA. International copyrights reserved in all countries. No part of this book may be reproduced in any form without written permission from the publisher.

Printed in the United States.

Cover Photo credits: Peter Arnold, Inc.
Interior Photo credits: Peter Arnold, Inc.

Edited by Lori Kinstad Pupeza

Library of Congress Cataloging-in-Publication Data

Kallen, Stuart A., 1955-
    Giant Pandas / Stuart A. Kallen
    p.   cm. -- (Bears)
    Summary: Briefly describes the physical characteristics, habitat, and behavior of China's giant pandas.
    Includes index.
    ISBN 1-56239-592-0
    1. Giant panda--Juvenile literature. [1. Giant panda. 2. Pandas.] I. Title. II. Series: Kallen, Stuart A., 1955-   Bears
    QL737.C214K34   1998
    599.74'443--dc20   95-52342
                                  CIP
                                  AC

Contents

The Giant Panda and Its Family

Giant Panda bears are **mammals**. Like humans, they breathe air with lungs, are **warm blooded**, and **nurse** their young with milk.

Bears first **evolved** around 40 million years ago. They were small, meat-eating, tree-climbing animals. The early bears were related to coyotes, wolves, foxes, raccoons, and even dogs. Today, there are eight different **species** of bear. They live in 50 countries on 3 **continents**.

The giant panda first roamed through eastern China. The ancient Chinese thought the panda had magic powers to cure disease and keep away evil spirits. The first live panda to be seen in America was in 1936.

Pandas are an **endangered species**. The lands where they live and the food they depend on are disappearing. There are only about 700 pandas left living in the wild. There are another 120 living in zoos, mostly in China.

A giant panda eating bamboo.

Size, Shape, and Color

The giant panda is large and slow. They are white with black eye patches, ears, legs, feet, chest, and shoulders. Adult pandas are about 6 feet (180 cm) long. They can weigh over 200 pounds (91 kg). Panda bears have heavily built bodies with short legs, necks, and tails. They have large heads with rounded ears. The pupils in a panda's eye are slit like a cat's, instead of round. The Panda's teeth have large, crushing molars that help them eat their favorite food: bamboo stalks.

Pandas have flexible front paws with a sixth **digit** that works like a human's thumb. This allows the panda to handle bamboo stems and leaves with ease. The panda's back feet lack the heel pad found in other bears. This gives them a clumsy looking walk. But pandas are able to move through rough **terrain** and dense forest very easily.

Unlike most bears, pandas do not **hibernate** in winter. They simply move to a lower **elevation**, where the climate is warmer.

A panda handling leaves with its six digit paw.

Where They Live

Pandas live in six small areas of China along the eastern side of the Tibetan Plateau. Hunting and logging has destroyed all of the areas where they used to live.

The giant pandas live in a cold, damp forest with an **elevation** between 4,000 and 11,000 feet (1,200 to 3,400 m). The bamboo that the pandas eat is found within this area.

More than half of the pandas today live in a chain of 12 reserves that have been set aside by the Chinese government. A study done by the World Wildlife Fund has shown that the number of pandas has shrunk by 200 in the last 10 years, leaving about 700 alive.

Opposite page: A panda near a stream in China.

Where Pandas
Are Found

Pandas are found in rural parts of south west China,
in an area called the Tibetan Plateau.

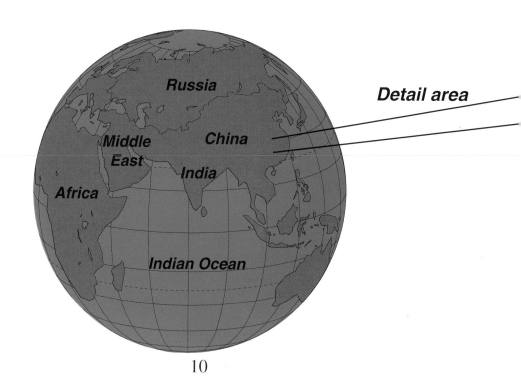

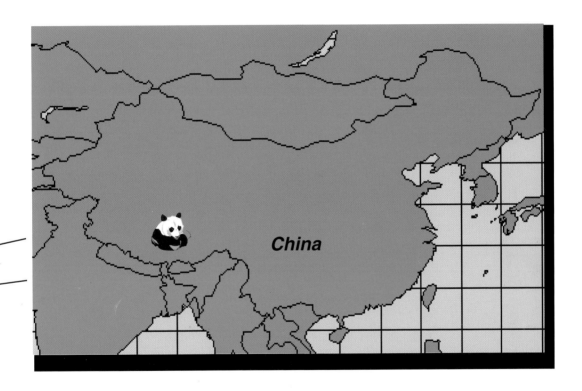

China

Senses

Like most bears, pandas are very smart animals that learn quickly. In Chinese zoos, some pandas are trained to do over 20 tricks, including riding a bicycle.

Because of their small eyes, there is a myth that bears cannot see well. But bears have good eyesight. They can tell the difference between colors and see well at night. They can spot moving objects at a far distance.

Giant pandas see and hear well but their sense of smell is their most important sense. Their keen sense of smell allows them to find mates, avoid humans, locate their **cubs**, and gather food.

Pandas will make noises when they are angry or afraid. They huff, snort, bark, yip, grunt, and squeal.

Opposite page: Pandas have small eyes but can still see very well.

Defense

Giant Pandas are slow, shy, and try to stay away from other animals. When not feeding, they lie around and sleep like cats. They will never run unless startled. They may trot, but never gallop like other bears. Pandas share their **habitat** with other pandas but rarely have face-to-face meetings. They are quiet loners.

Pandas usually eat only bamboo but sometimes eat meat. If they do attack another animal they will swat with their paws, lunge, and bite with their powerful jaws.

The only animals that will attack the panda are humans. Unlike other bears, pandas are poor climbers. If they are chased, they will try to climb up a tree. Females will climb trees to get away from males.

Opposite page: A panda sitting in the forest.

Food

Pandas like to eat the leaves and the stems of the bamboo plant. But they will eat meat if they can. They have been seen eating fish and rodents. They may even enter logging camps to steal meat from humans. Giant pandas will eat flowers like irises and crocuses. They also eat vines, horsetails, fir bark, and grass.

Their throats and stomachs have a tough lining that help them swallow and digest the sharp bamboo splinters. A panda needs to eat 45 pounds (20 kg) of bamboo a day to survive. In the spring pandas move to lower **elevations** to eat fresh bamboo shoots growing out of the ground.

Sometimes all the bamboo in an area will die at once. This causes great harm to the pandas living there. New bamboo seedlings need 10 years to grow

large enough to become good panda food. Farming and villages have cut into the panda's **habitat**.

A panda looking for food.

Babies

The giant panda does not breed well. They can not have babies until they are seven years old. Pandas are pregnant for 3 to 6 months. Newborn pandas are tiny, weighing only 3 to 5 ounces (90 to 140 kg). The mother panda gives birth in a cave or hollow tree in late August or early September.

The **cubs** are blind, toothless, and 6 inches (15 cm) long. They are pink, hairless, and helpless. But they have a loud cry that can be heard over 300 feet (90 m) away.

The mother panda cradles the newborn in her front paws for the first three weeks. She sits upright and **nurses** her baby like a human mother. After a few weeks, black fur appears and the cub's eyes open. The cub begins to walk and eat bamboo. By the time they are one year old, panda cubs weigh 75

pounds (35 kg). They usually leave their mothers after one or two years.

Pandas are dying out in the wild. They do not breed well in zoos. If their habitat is not saved, pandas won't live in the wild by the year 2000.

A young panda.

Giant Panda Facts

Scientific Name: *Ursus melanoleucas.*

Average Size: Between 5 and 6 feet (160 to 180 cm) long. They may weigh over 200 pounds (91 kg). Adult males may be 10 to 20 percent larger than females.

Where They're Found: The eastern edge of the Tibetan Plateau in China.

Opposite page: A giant panda walking through a forest.

Glossary

continent (KAHN-tih-nent) - one of the seven main land masses: Europe, Asia, Africa, North America, South America, Australia, and Antarctica.

cub - a baby bear.

digit - a finger or toe.

elevation - the altitude of a place above sea level.

endangered species - any type of plant or animal that is threatened with extinction.

evolve - for a species to develop or change over millions of years.

habitat - the place where an animal or plant naturally lives.

hibernate - to spend the winter in a deep sleep.

mammal - a class of animals, including humans, that have hair and feed their young milk.

nurse - to feed a young animal or child milk from the mother's breast.

prey - an animal hunted and captured for food.

species (SPEE-sees) - a group of related living things that have the same basic characteristics.

terrain - a tract of land.

warm blooded - an animal whose body temperature remains the same and warmer than the outside air or temperature.

Index